Series 536

THE LADYBIRD
BOOK OF PETS

By
GEORGE CANSDALE

Colour Illustrations by
EDWARD OSMOND

Publishers: Wills & Hepworth Ltd., Loughborough

First published 1957　　*Printed in England*

Donkey

Donkeys are clever, patient animals. The first donkeys came from the rocky deserts of North Africa, so they are sure-footed and hardy, too. They were our friends long before there were any tame horses, and in the days of Abraham they were a great help in carrying all the baggage on long, hard journeys.

Nowadays, we do not often see donkeys at work, but in Ireland they still pull little carts along, while at Carisbrooke Castle, on the Isle of Wight, you can see a patient donkey walking inside a huge wheel to draw up water from the well.

And, of course, every boy and girl loves to ride on a donkey on the golden sands at the seaside.

7214·0094 9

Pony

Most of us are not lucky enough to have a pony of our own, but what fun it is to ride one, especially when we can join our friends at the Pony Club.

There are several kinds, such as the Exmoor, New Forest and Welsh ponies, and best known of all, the tiny Shetland pony from that part of Scotland after which it is named. Most ponies grow heavy coats that keep them warm and have long, thick tails.

Ponies and horses are always measured in ' hands ' of just four inches each; so a Shetland pony of ' ten hands ' is three feet four inches tall at the shoulder.

Both ponies and horses like to eat a lump of sugar, and the proper way to offer this is on the flat, open hand, then they will not bite your fingers by mistake.

Fox Terrier

Many years ago fox terriers really lived up to their name and, being full of courage, were used to make foxes come out of their holes. Those early fox terriers were all kinds of colours and shapes. They had rather short legs so that they could follow foxes underground.

The fox terriers which you see here would not be much good for chasing foxes, but they are very handsome dogs. The pedigree fox terrier has a fine, smooth coat, which is mostly white with just a little black or brown colouring. Its tail is short and the legs are rather long.

The other fox terrier is about the same size, but has a rough coat; this one is called the wire-haired terrier.

Spaniel

Spaniels are real English dogs and they were special favourites of King Charles II nearly 300 years ago. They have always been sporting dogs, loving to help their masters in the fields and woods, and even swimming in the coldest water.

The cocker spaniel is the best known kind to-day and is popular in towns as well as in the country. It has lovely, brown eyes and fluffy ears as long as its head. Cockers can be almost any colour, but they are generally golden, black or black and white.

The other kinds of spaniels are much bigger dogs and they all have to work. They are called springer, clumber and Sussex spaniels. Still another kind is called the Irish water spaniel; this is the tallest of them all and its curly coat makes it look like a big poodle.

Toy Poodle

Poodles are a very old breed of dog. They are often called French poodles, but many people think they really came from Germany. The toy poodle is one of the smallest kind of dogs, being not more than twelve inches high, and so it is often a favourite pet in small houses.

All poodles are clever dogs and at one time they were much used in hunting. With their thick, curly coats they did not mind going into water to fetch the ducks which had been shot. Poodles are good at learning tricks and are often trained to perform in circuses.

Many poodles are clipped as this one is, but for Shows they have what is called the "lion clip", with lots of long fur on the head and front of the body, and the rest of it clipped short.

Dachshund

Dachshunds are a very popular breed of dogs. These began as working dogs in Germany many years ago. The dachshund's short legs allow it to follow a badger right down its hole, or "set", as it is called. Perhaps our pets have not quite the strength and courage to go after badgers, but they make fine house dogs and the smooth-haired kind are the easiest dogs to keep in good condition.

Another kind of dachshund is the long-haired dog, which has a wonderfully soft, silky coat. It is smooth on the back and long on the sides; the legs and tail are " feathered " as they are in the lovely, big retriever.

Mongrel Dog

If a dog does not belong to one of the many well-known breeds we sometimes call it a mongrel, but a mongrel can be just as faithful and good a pal as any other kind, and is usually a very good watch-dog.

Dogs have been friendly with mankind for longer than any other animals, and always enjoy living with us as much as we like having them.

If we keep a dog we must look after it properly. It needs suitable food at regular mealtimes; a bowl of clean water always ready, its very own corner and bed to sleep in; and plenty of exercise, though some dogs need much more than others.

Carrier Pigeon

Pigeons are the only birds which are of real service to us. They can carry a written message, enclosed in a tiny tube strapped to the leg, more quickly than any other creature.

They cannot, of course, take a message just anywhere, but only back to their own homes. The pigeons are taught to do this by being taken in special baskets farther and farther away from their home lofts and then set free to fly back again. When they have been well trained they can make return flights from even 500 miles away.

Pigeons first carried messages over 2,000 years ago, and even nowadays are used to carry very important messages at times.

Carrier pigeons are of various colours, but in shape they are most like their wild cousins, the rock doves, which are also expert fliers.

Fantail Pigeon

At one time all tame pigeons were rather like their wild cousins, the rock doves. Now there are many quite different breeds.

The carrier pigeons are the working birds, strong and fast-flying, while the white fantails are of the ornamental kind. They certainly do look very lovely as they feed on the lawn or rest on the roof-tops. Fantails can fly around the garden, but they are of no use for long or fast-flying journeys.

All tame pigeons like to eat green vegetables, but they feed mostly on seeds, such as maize, wheat and field peas. These seeds are very hard, so they also have to swallow small bits of hard stone to help grind them up in their crops, or stomachs.

Dove

The proper name for the tame dove is the Barbary turtle dove. It comes from North Africa, and is a cousin of the lovely turtle dove with the soft voice, that visits us in summer time.

It was one of the very first birds that became tame and is mentioned many times in the Bible. The dove is about the same size as the tame pigeon and its pretty plumage is very pale, with a tiny black collar.

Like all members of the pigeon family, the turtle dove lays just two pure white eggs and feeds its babies with food which it specially prepares in its own crop. After about a fortnight the baby doves begin to get their proper feathers and two weeks later they can fly.

Tabby Cat

What a lot of nursery rhymes there are about cats! Perhaps you like this one:

" Pussy cat, pussy cat,
Where have you been ?
I've been to London
To look at the Queen."

Or do you prefer:

" I love little pussy
Her coat is so warm."

Nowadays, our cats live mostly in our houses and make themselves very much at home; but many, many years ago there were no tame cats. Then they were all hunters, living in the woods and fields of Egypt. When mice came to steal the Egyptians' corn, the wild cats came to catch them and stayed on and became friendly.

The very first tame cat was quite like this tabby in the picture.

Siamese Cat

The first Siamese cats are said to have been brought to England from Siam, where they were looked upon as royal animals. These cats are very smart, with pale bodies and dark feet, faces and ears; and they also have beautiful, blue eyes.

In some ways Siamese cats seem more like dogs. For instance, they like to be with people, and some even wear little collars and leads when they are taken out for walks. They do not ' meow ' like other cats, but almost seem to be talking to us.

Many Siamese cats seem to like watching television, especially when animals are being shown on the screen.

Goldfish

Chinese people were keeping goldfish many hundreds of years ago. The wild goldfish was a kind of golden carp, like the carp we have in our ponds and lakes; but soon the Chinese fish-keepers managed to breed more brightly coloured fishes, some of them with long fins and tails.

A goldfish bowl must not be more than half full of water, nor must it be over-crowded; this means that only one very small goldfish should live in a bowl; if you keep more than one you should, if possible, have a small tank. You need not change the water, but you must take out the dirt from the bottom by using a little glass tube.

If you give goldfish too much food some will be left over, and this spoils the water.

Dutch Rabbit

Although there are now many different kinds of tame rabbits, they have all been bred from wild rabbits like those we see in the fields and woods. When fully grown the tiniest of all weigh under three pounds, but the biggest weigh over twenty pounds.

The smartly patterned Dutch rabbit is a children's favourite, with its smooth coat of white and some other colour, usually black or chocolate.

Some people advise giving water or milk, but many rabbits seldom drink if they have plenty of fresh green food. If you have a lawn you may be able to let your rabbits have a run on it during the summer.

Angora Rabbit

This big puff-ball of a rabbit gets its name from the Angora goat, which gives such beautiful soft wool, but underneath its thick coat it is just like any other rabbit.

Although it is not more difficult to feed than any other kind of rabbit, its coat needs a lot of attention and must be groomed every day.

Most Angora rabbits are kept for their long, soft coats, which are clipped or plucked regularly and sold as wool. One rabbit can give about eight ounces in a year. This is first spun into yarn and then knitted into clothes, such as little jerseys, berets, gloves and babies' bonnets.

Chinchilla Rabbit

The true Chinchilla is a delightful little animal that lives in the mountains of South America. It has a stiff, bushy tail and probably the softest fur in the whole world.

This rabbit gets its name because its fur is coloured like the true Chinchilla's but, like the Angora, it is just an ordinary rabbit under its thick coat.

Whatever kind of rabbit you have for a pet, please look after it carefully. Clean out the corner every day where the droppings are left, and twice a week clean the whole hutch thoroughly.

All rabbits love green food and eat lots of it, but it is best not to give any lettuce at all. Be careful in winter time not to give rabbits any leaves which have been frost-bitten.

Guinea-Pig

When the Spanish sailors first visited Peru over 400 years ago, the Inca people were keeping some strange little pets. They had no tails, ate vegetable food, and lived in little burrows. When the colonists came back home they brought some of these guinea-pigs with them—or cavies, as some folk call them.

Guinea-pigs need the same kind of hutch as rabbits, with a snug sleeping place away from draughts. They eat a mixture of green stuff, roots and dry food, such as crusts, bran, or biscuit meal. Three to seven babies are born at a time, and they run around and start nibbling almost at once, but they generally go on having some milk from their mother for about three weeks.

Canary

Although we may keep other pet birds, the canary is still the best singer. The first canaries came from the Canary Islands near the west coast of Africa, but these were more green than yellow.

All canaries may look rather alike, but there are several kinds. Some are all yellow, others have darker markings, while others have green feathers.

" Roller " canaries make the best singers. These have been taught their songs by older expert singing birds.

Canaries are like finches and have strong beaks for cracking little seeds. They also enjoy green plants like dandelion, groundsel or spinach.

See that your canary always has clean water and that its cage is never in a draught.

Budgerigar

The first budgerigars were brought to this country from Australia nearly 100 years ago. Wild budgerigars are mostly green, with some yellow on the head and other dark markings. Since they became tame, many colours have been bred and budgies to-day are all shades of green, blue, and yellow, with various markings, too, while some of them are even white.

The budgie is also called the grass parakeet, which just means that it is a long-tailed, little parrot, and it feeds on grass seeds. Although these pets do well on a mixture of dry seeds, they enjoy some fresh green food and soon finish off a head of flowering grass.

Remember to give them some cuttle bone and a block of mineral grit.

Goat

Do you ever call anybody "a silly goat"? Goats are actually not at all silly. They are experts at running and jumping on steep rocks we could not even climb. Some even learn to climb trees to get the leaves.

Goats have been serving mankind for a very long time. Abraham and his people had big flocks of them to provide milk and meat. The skins were made into leather, from which they made many useful things, including sandals and water bottles.

Now there are several different kinds of tame goats, but all of them have come from the wild goats living on the hills in Greece. We keep goats mostly for their milk, and this is delicious, especially if the goats are well fed on hay and leaves.

Golden Hamster

This is the newest pet of all and in some ways the nicest. It takes up little room, and if you clean out its box properly it does not smell.

There are several different kinds of hamsters. This one comes from Syria, in the near East, where it makes its home in burrows. In summer it carries seeds home in its cheek pouches to make a store for the winter.

Remember to give your golden hamster some fresh green food like lettuce; it likes fruit, too, such as apple peelings. If you can find any insects it will eat them greedily. Do not be surprised if the food pot is emptied at once; the hamster has probably carried it all to its nest.

Hedgehog

What a prickly bundle is our hedgehog! When it rolls into a tight ball, head safely tucked inside, it is safe from most enemies. It belongs to the same family as the little shrews and the burrowing moles, and they all eat small creatures like worms, slugs, snails and insects.

Hedgehogs do not make good house pets, but it is fun to be friends with one in the garden. A hedgehog helps the gardener by killing the slugs, preferring to find its own food, although it may learn to come for a saucer of milk. Hedgehogs sleep by day and are active at night. They hide away fast asleep in cold weather, but they come out to feed on warm winter days.

Tortoise

There are many kinds of tortoises, but our pets come from Mediterranean countries and are called Greek tortoises. They eat only vegetable food. Some like one thing best and some another; so try them with food like lettuce and cabbage, dandelion, clover and buttercup leaves; rose leaves and petals, and tomatoes.

When winter comes, let your tortoise go to sleep until the late spring. Pack it in leaf-mould and then put it away in a shed or garage protected from heavy frost. When the tortoise awakens it is often rather drowsy and may not feed for a week or two. If its eyelids are stuck together, bathe them with eye lotion.

White Mouse

Although we often talk about " white " mice, there are really many different coloured ones, and some of these are very pretty.

The first home of these mice was far away in Asia, but instead of staying in the jungles they moved into the villages and towns and soon became house mice, which is now their proper name. They gradually spread to other countries and now they are everywhere. Mice were first tamed as pets several hundreds of years ago.

It is the male mice that smell most, so if you keep only one it is better to have a female. Feed your mice on clipped oats, with a little canary seed; one will eat about a dessertspoonful every day. Also every day give a small piece of stale bread soaked slightly in milk.

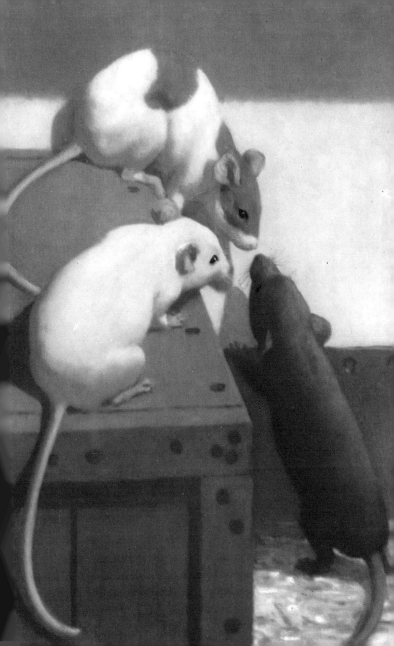

Series 536